# START SELLING WITHOUT INVENTORY

## *Build Your Dropshipping Empire*

## Dack Douglas

**Icon Publications Limited**

# CONTENTS

# FOREWORD

Welcome to "Start Selling Without Inventory: Build Your Dropshipping Empire." In this book, we embark on a journey to explore the ins and outs of building a successful Dropshipping business. Whether you're a seasoned entrepreneur or a budding enthusiast, this guide aims to equip you with the essential knowledge and strategies to start and thrive in the e-commerce landscape.

Through these pages, you will uncover the art of product selection, understanding market trends, and mastering the art of customer engagement. I believe that with the right mindset, dedication, and the insights shared here, you can turn your aspirations into a reality.

Dropshipping offers a unique opportunity to bridge the gap between creativity and commerce, enabling anyone to venture into the world of online business without the traditional barriers. As you dive into this book, I encourage you to embrace the challenges and embrace the rewards that come with building your own venture.

Remember, success in Dropshipping is not merely about making transactions but creating a meaningful connection with your customers. Empathy, innovation, and adaptability are the keys that will unlock the doors to growth and prosperity.

Let this book be your guide as you embark on your Dropshipping journey. Embrace every chapter, apply the knowledge shared, and let your entrepreneurial spirit flourish. I wish you the best of luck and immense fulfillment in your pursuit of building a thriving and impactful Dropshipping business.

Here's to your success and the incredible possibilities that lie ahead!

# INTRODUCTION

In a vast and ever-evolving digital landscape, the potential for e-commerce success is boundless. If you've ever dreamed of starting your own online business, embracing the world of dropshipping could be your gateway to financial independence. **"Start Selling Without Inventory: Build Your Dropshipping Empire,"** is a comprehensive guide that will equip aspiring entrepreneurs like you with the knowledge, strategies, and practical steps needed to embark on a successful dropshipping journey.

# START SELLING WITHOUT INVENTORY: BUILD YOUR DROPSHIPPING EMPIRE

# CHAPTER 1: UNDERSTANDING DROPSHIPPING

## Defining Dropshipping And Its Advantages

Dropshipping is a modern e-commerce business model that empowers entrepreneurs to operate without the need for large inventory holdings. In this innovative approach, the retailer partners with suppliers or wholesalers who handle the product storage, packaging, and shipment directly to customers. As a result, the retailer doesn't need to stock items physically, and each order is fulfilled seamlessly by the supplier.

Advantages of Dropshipping:

1. Minimal Capital Investment: Dropshipping eliminates the need for significant upfront investments in inventory, allowing entrepreneurs to start their businesses with relatively low financial risk. This accessibility has opened doors for aspiring individuals to explore the world of e-commerce.

2. Wide Product Variety: The dropshipping model enables retailers to offer an extensive array of products without worrying about storage limitations. This versatility allows businesses to cater to diverse customer demands and tap into various niche markets.

3. Flexibility and Scalability: Dropshipping liberates entrepreneurs from the burdens of warehousing and order fulfillment logistics. As sales grow, the business can effortlessly scale up without the hassle of managing increased inventory demands or handling shipping complexities.

4. Reduced Operational Complexity: With dropshipping, retailers can concentrate on the core aspects of their business, such as marketing, customer support, and brand development, without the need to handle product handling and shipping logistics.

5. Global Reach: The online nature of dropshipping facilitates the ability to reach customers worldwide. This geographical flexibility provides businesses with access to a broader audience, unlocking the potential for international growth and increased revenue streams.

6. Testing and Innovation: Dropshipping empowers entrepreneurs to experiment with new products and ideas without committing to large quantities upfront. This testing environment fosters innovation and agility, allowing businesses to adapt swiftly to market trends and customer preferences.

7. Low Overhead Costs: Since dropshipping eliminates the need for physical storage space and associated expenses, businesses can maintain lower overhead costs. This cost-effectiveness allows for greater profitability and potential for reinvestment in business growth.

*In conclusion, dropshipping stands as an enticing and rewarding business model that has revolutionized the e-commerce landscape. Entrepreneurs can leverage its advantages to forge successful ventures, all while embracing flexibility, innovation, and the potential for global reach in the ever-evolving world of online commerce.*

# Exploring The Evolving E-Commerce Industry

The most effective approach to delve into the dynamic e-commerce industry with dropshipping is to adopt a three-fold strategy: Educate, Innovate, and Collaborate.

1. Educate: Start by immersing yourself in the world of e-commerce and dropshipping. Take the time to research and understand the fundamental principles, trends, and best practices in the field. Read books, follow industry experts and successful dropshippers, and explore case studies to gain valuable insights.

2. Innovate: To thrive in the evolving e-commerce landscape, innovation is key. Identify gaps in the market, explore emerging product trends, and seek unique ways to offer value to customers. Embrace creativity and be willing to experiment with novel marketing techniques, user experiences, and customer engagement strategies.

3. Collaborate: Building meaningful connections in the dropshipping community can be invaluable. Engage with fellow entrepreneurs, suppliers, and experts to exchange knowledge, share experiences, and seek guidance. Collaborating with others can open doors to new opportunities, inspire fresh ideas, and create a support network for your business.

*By combining education, innovation, and collaboration, you can position yourself as an agile and informed player in the evolving e-commerce industry. This holistic approach will empower you to navigate challenges, capitalize on opportunities, and embark on a successful dropshipping journey that stands the test of time. Remember, adaptability and a thirst for learning will be your greatest assets in this ever-changing landscape.*

# Debunking Common Myths And Misconceptions

Debunking common myths and misconceptions about dropshipping requires shedding light on the realities of this business model. Here are the key points to address:

1. Myth: Dropshipping guarantees instant success and effortless profits. Reality: While dropshipping offers exciting opportunities, it is not a get-rich-quick scheme. Building a successful dropshipping business requires dedication, market research, and strategic planning. Like any business, it takes time and effort to see significant results.

2. Myth: Dropshipping doesn't require any investment. Reality: While dropshipping requires lower upfront costs compared to traditional retail models, it still involves initial investments in setting up a professional website, marketing, and customer acquisition. Additionally, success may require investing in premium tools or courses to enhance your skills and knowledge.

3. Myth: Dropshipping is saturated, and there's no room for newcomers. Reality: While dropshipping has grown in popularity, there are still numerous untapped niches and unique product opportunities. Finding the right niche and offering value to a specific target audience can set you apart from the competition.

4. Myth: Customers won't trust dropshipped products. Reality: Trust lies in the quality of products and customer service. By partnering with reliable suppliers and providing excellent customer support, you can establish trust and credibility with your audience.

5. Myth: Dropshipping is entirely hands-off and automated. Reality: While automation tools can streamline certain aspects of dropshipping, successful entrepreneurs actively engage in their business. This includes monitoring inventory levels, maintaining supplier relationships, and consistently optimizing marketing strategies.

6. Myth: Only expensive products lead to substantial profits. Reality: Profitability depends on various factors, not just product prices. Higher-priced items may yield more profit per sale, but lower-priced products can generate consistent sales volume and still be profitable.

7. Myth: Dropshipping doesn't require any marketing effort. Reality: Marketing is vital for any business, including dropshipping. Effective marketing strategies are essential for driving traffic to your website, converting visitors into customers, and building a loyal customer base.

8. Myth: Customer complaints are not your responsibility as a dropshipper. Reality: As the retailer, you are responsible for the customer experience. Handling customer complaints and inquiries with professionalism is crucial for maintaining a positive reputation and fostering long-term relationships with customers.

*By addressing these myths and providing a realistic perspective on dropshipping, aspiring entrepreneurs can make informed decisions, set appropriate expectations, and approach this business model with a clear understanding of its potential and challenges.*

* * *

# CHAPTER 2: NICHE SELECTION AND MARKET RESEARCH

## Unveiling The Power Of Niche Selection

Unveiling the power of niche selection is the gateway to unlocking the true potential of your dropshipping business. Here's how you can harness its strength:

1. Passion and Interest: Start by exploring your own passions and interests. Selecting a niche that resonates with you will fuel your motivation and commitment to dive deeper into the market. Remember, your enthusiasm will shine through in your marketing efforts and customer interactions.

2. Research and Analysis: Conduct thorough market research to identify emerging trends, customer preferences, and potential demand for products within your chosen niche. Understanding the competitive landscape and target audience will help you position your business effectively.

3. Uniqueness and Value Proposition: Look for opportunities to offer something unique within your niche. Differentiate your business by providing exceptional value, whether it's through exclusive products,

exceptional customer service, or innovative solutions to common pain points.

4. Profitability and Feasibility: While passion is essential, ensure that your chosen niche also holds the promise of profitability. Evaluate profit margins, shipping costs, and market size to gauge the feasibility of your dropshipping venture.

5. Evergreen vs. Trending: Consider whether your niche is evergreen (timeless and consistently in demand) or based on trending products. While trending items can lead to quick sales, an evergreen niche provides stability and long-term growth potential.

6. Audience Targeting: Understand your target audience's needs, interests, and pain points. Tailor your marketing messages and product offerings to align with their preferences, which will enhance customer engagement and boost sales.

7. Supplier Reliability: Partner with reliable suppliers who can consistently deliver quality products and timely shipping. Reliable suppliers ensure a positive customer experience, which is crucial for building trust and repeat business.

8. Scalability: Think about the scalability of your chosen niche. While starting small can be prudent, ensure that your niche has the potential for growth and expansion over time.

9. Data-Driven Approach: Utilize analytics tools to track and measure your business's performance. Analyzing data will provide insights into customer behavior, product popularity, and areas for improvement, empowering you to make informed decisions.

10. Adaptability and Evolution: The e-commerce landscape is ever-changing. Stay open to adapting your niche selection strategy based on market shifts and customer demands. Embrace flexibility and continue to innovate as you progress in your dropshipping journey.

*By unveiling the power of niche selection through passion, research, uniqueness, and adaptability, you can position your dropshipping business for success. Remember that niche selection is not just a one-time decision; it requires ongoing evaluation and optimization to stay ahead in the competitive e-commerce arena.*

# Conducting Thorough Market Research

Conducting thorough market research is essential for the success of your dropshipping business. Here are some original ways to gather valuable insights:

1. Online Forums and Communities: Engage with niche-specific online forums, social media groups, and communities. Observe discussions, questions, and pain points raised by potential customers. This real-time interaction will help you understand their needs and preferences.

2. Competitor Analysis: Study your competitors' dropshipping stores within your chosen niche. Analyze their product offerings, pricing strategies, customer reviews, and marketing techniques. Identify gaps in their approach and explore opportunities to differentiate your business.

3. Customer Surveys: Create surveys and questionnaires to gather direct feedback from your target audience. Ask about their preferences, shopping habits, and pain points. Incentivize participation to encourage a higher response rate.

4. Keyword Research: Utilize keyword research tools to identify popular search terms related to your niche. This will give you insights into what potential customers are actively searching for online, guiding your product selection and content creation.

5. Trend Analysis: Keep a close eye on industry trends and emerging products. Platforms like Google Trends and social media can reveal the popularity of certain products and concepts. Stay ahead of the curve by incorporating trending items into your offerings.

6. Supplier Partnerships: Build relationships with potential suppliers and manufacturers. Engage in conversations to understand their product catalogs, pricing structures, and shipping capabilities. A reliable supplier is crucial for the smooth operation of your dropshipping business.

7. Influencer Insights: Collaborate with influencers or bloggers who cater to your target audience. They can provide valuable insights into customer preferences and help you reach a broader audience through their established networks.

8. Demographic Research: Study the demographics of your target audience, including age, gender, location, and interests. This information will enable you to tailor your marketing efforts to resonate with your ideal customers.

9. Product Reviews: Analyze customer reviews for products within your niche, whether on e-commerce platforms or other review websites. Understanding what customers appreciate or dislike about similar products can guide your product selection.

10. Test Marketing Campaigns: Run small-scale marketing campaigns for potential products to gauge customer interest and response. A/B test different strategies to determine the most effective marketing approaches.

*By employing these original market research methods, you'll gain comprehensive insights into your target audience, competitors, and product viability. The knowledge you gather will empower you to make informed decisions, shape your dropshipping business strategy, and create a customer-centric brand that stands out in the competitive e-commerce landscape.*

# Identifying Profitable Product Categories

Identifying profitable product categories for your dropshipping business requires a blend of strategic analysis and market intuition. Here are original steps to guide you:
1. Niche Exploration: Research and explore various niches that align with your interests and passions. Look for niches with a strong demand and untapped potential. Seek out unique subcategories that might not be oversaturated in the market.

2. Market Trend Analysis: Stay up-to-date with the latest market trends and consumer behavior. Analyze industry reports, news, and social media to identify emerging products and growing trends. Stay ahead of the curve by offering products that are in high demand.

3. Keyword Research: Use keyword research tools to identify relevant search terms and phrases related to potential product categories. High search volumes indicate a strong interest in those products, which could translate into higher sales potential.

4. Profit Margin Evaluation: Assess the profit margins of products within your potential categories. Look for items with reasonable costs and competitive selling prices. High-profit margins will contribute to a financially viable dropshipping business.

5. Seasonal and Evergreen Considerations: Distinguish between seasonal products with fluctuating demand and evergreen items with consistent year-round interest. A mix of both can provide stability and growth opportunities throughout the year.

6. Competition Analysis: Study competitors selling products in your chosen categories. Analyze their strengths, weaknesses, and pricing strategies. Identify gaps in the market that you can fill or unique selling points that can set your business apart.

7. Customer Persona Creation: Develop detailed customer personas for your target audience. Understand their preferences, pain points, and purchasing behavior. Tailor your product selection to meet their specific needs and desires.

8. Supplier Reliability: Partner with reliable suppliers who offer quality products and efficient shipping services. A trustworthy supplier ensures a positive customer experience and reduces the risk of potential issues.

9. Test Products: Test potential products on a small scale to gauge customer interest and demand. Utilize social media ads or email marketing to measure customer response before committing to larger orders.

10. Monitor Market Shifts: Stay adaptable and be prepared to adjust your product categories as market trends and consumer preferences evolve. Continuously monitor performance metrics and customer feedback to fine-tune your offerings.

*By combining data-driven research with your intuition and understanding of your target audience, you can identify profitable product categories for your dropshipping business. Remember, finding the right mix of niche specificity and market demand will lay the foundation for sustainable growth and long-term success in the competitive e-commerce landscape.*

* * *

# CHAPTER 3: BUILDING A STRONG FOUNDATION

## Establishing Your Brand Identity

Establishing a compelling brand identity for your dropshipping business is a crucial step in standing out amidst the competition and building a loyal customer base. Here's an original guide to help you create a strong brand identity:

1. Define Your Brand Values: Start by clarifying your core brand values and mission. What do you stand for? What unique attributes will set your business apart? Craft a clear and authentic brand message that resonates with your target audience.

2. Create a Memorable Logo: Design a distinctive and memorable logo that embodies your brand's essence. Your logo will serve as the visual representation of your business and leave a lasting impression on customers.

3. Craft a Unique Voice: Develop a consistent brand voice that reflects your personality and values. Whether it's professional, playful, or informative, your brand voice should align with your target audience's preferences and communicate your message effectively.

4. Choose a Captivating Name: Select a brand name that is easy to remember, spell, and pronounce. Ensure it aligns with your niche and overall brand image. A well-chosen name can leave a lasting impression on potential customers.

5. Design a Cohesive Website: Create a visually appealing and user-friendly website that reflects your brand's personality and showcases your products effectively. Use consistent colors, fonts, and imagery to reinforce your brand identity.

6. Tell Your Story: Share your brand's story and journey with your customers. People connect with authentic narratives, so tell them why you started your business and how it addresses their needs or desires.

7. Engage on Social Media: Use social media platforms to interact with your audience regularly. Post engaging content that aligns with your brand values and sparks conversations. Respond to comments and messages promptly to build a community around your brand.

8. Offer Exceptional Customer Service: Deliver outstanding customer service to create a positive brand perception. Go above and beyond to address customer inquiries and resolve issues promptly and professionally.

9. Utilize Packaging as Branding: If possible, customize your packaging with your logo and brand colors. Thoughtful packaging can leave a lasting impression on customers and reinforce your brand identity.

10. Collaborate and Sponsor: Collaborate with influencers or other brands in your niche to expand your reach and strengthen your brand presence. Sponsor relevant events or causes that align with your brand values to showcase your commitment to social responsibility.

*Consistency is key throughout all aspects of your brand identity. By infusing your values, voice, and visuals into every interaction with customers, you'll build a cohesive and authentic brand that*

# Setting Up A Professional Online Store

Setting up a professional online store for your dropshipping business requires careful planning and attention to detail. Here's an original step-by-step guide to help you create an impressive e-commerce platform:

1. Choose the Right E-commerce Platform: Select a user-friendly and feature-rich e-commerce platform that aligns with your needs. Platforms like Shopify, WooCommerce, or BigCommerce offer intuitive interfaces and a range of customizable templates to create a professional online store.

2. Domain Name and Hosting: Register a domain name that reflects your brand and is easy for customers to remember. Secure reliable hosting to ensure your online store loads quickly and remains accessible to visitors at all times.

3. Mobile-Optimized Design: Optimize your online store for mobile devices. With the majority of internet traffic coming from mobile users, a responsive design ensures a seamless shopping experience across various devices.

4. Compelling Product Pages: Create product pages that showcase your products with high-quality images, detailed descriptions, and clear pricing information. Use persuasive copywriting to highlight the benefits and unique selling points of each product.

5. Secure Payment Gateways: Integrate secure payment gateways to provide customers with a safe and hassle-free checkout process. Offer multiple payment options to accommodate various preferences.

6. Implement User Reviews and Ratings: Encourage customer reviews and ratings on your product pages. Positive reviews build trust and credibility, influencing potential customers to make a purchase.

7. Seamless Navigation: Organize your store's navigation intuitively, making it easy for visitors to find products, categories, and important information. Implement search functionality to enable quick product searches.

8. Build Trust with Policies: Display clear and transparent policies for shipping, returns, and privacy. Instill trust in your customers by showcasing your commitment to excellent service and data security.

9. Implement Live Chat Support: Offer live chat support to assist customers in real-time with their inquiries or concerns. Prompt and personalized assistance can enhance customer satisfaction and lead to increased sales.

10. Test and Optimize: Continuously test different elements of your online store, such as call-to-action buttons, images, and product positioning. Use analytics tools to gather data and optimize your store's performance for better conversions.

11. Brand Consistency: Maintain consistency with your brand's colors, logo, and messaging throughout your online store. A cohesive brand image reinforces your identity and helps customers recognize your brand easily.

*By following these original steps, you can create a professional online store that not only showcases your dropshipping products effectively but also provides a seamless and enjoyable shopping experience for your customers. A well-designed and user-friendly online store will be the foundation of your dropshipping business's success in the competitive e-commerce landscape.*

## Selecting The Right E-Commerce Platform

Selecting the right e-commerce platform for your dropshipping business is a critical decision that can impact your success. Here's an original guide to help you make the best choice:

1. Define Your Business Needs: Start by clarifying your business requirements and objectives. Consider factors like product range, scalability, budget, and level of customization needed. Understanding your needs will guide your platform selection.

2. User-Friendly Interface: Opt for an e-commerce platform with an intuitive and user-friendly interface. This will make it easier for you to manage your store and navigate the backend without extensive technical knowledge.

3. Dropshipping Integration: Ensure that the platform supports seamless integration with dropshipping apps or extensions. Look for pre-built integrations with popular dropshipping platforms to simplify product sourcing and order fulfillment.

4. Payment Gateway Options: Choose a platform that offers multiple payment gateway options to accommodate your target audience's preferences. The availability of trusted payment gateways enhances the checkout experience for customers.

5. Mobile Responsiveness: In today's mobile-driven world, select a platform that offers mobile-responsive templates. This ensures your online store looks and functions optimally on various devices, providing a positive shopping experience for mobile users.

6. Security and Hosting: Prioritize security features and reliable hosting. Look for platforms that offer SSL encryption and secure data handling to safeguard your customers' information during transactions.

7. Customization and Design: Assess the level of customization the platform allows. Select a platform that offers flexibility in design, so you can tailor your online store to match your brand identity and create a unique shopping experience.

8. App Ecosystem: Consider the availability of apps and plugins in the platform's ecosystem. Access to a variety of apps can extend the functionality of your store, helping you implement marketing, analytics, and customer support tools.

9. Customer Support: Evaluate the quality and availability of customer support provided by the platform. Reliable and responsive customer support will be essential in case you encounter technical issues or need assistance.

10. Cost and Pricing Structure: Compare the pricing plans of different platforms and consider how they align with your budget and business goals. Factor in transaction fees, hosting costs, and additional expenses when making your decision.

11. Reviews and Feedback: Research user reviews and feedback from other dropshippers who have used the platform. Learning

from others' experiences can provide valuable insights into the platform's performance and reliability.

> *By considering these original factors, you can confidently select the right e-commerce platform for your dropshipping business. Take your time to weigh the pros and cons of each option, and remember that the ideal platform will cater to your unique needs, support your growth, and enhance your customers' shopping experience.*

* * *

# CHAPTER 4: SOURCING PRODUCTS AND SUPPLIERS

## Identifying Reliable Suppliers

Identifying reliable suppliers is crucial for the smooth operation of your dropshipping business. Here are original steps to help you find trustworthy partners:

1. Thorough Research: Start by conducting extensive research on potential suppliers. Utilize online directories, industry-specific platforms, and trade shows to identify suppliers within your niche.

2. Contact Multiple Suppliers: Reach out to multiple suppliers to gather information about their products, shipping times, and policies. Comparing multiple options will help you make an informed decision.

3. Request Samples: Request product samples from shortlisted suppliers to assess the quality of their products and packaging. Hands-on evaluation will give you firsthand experience of what your customers will receive.

4. Check Reputation and Reviews: Look for customer reviews and ratings of suppliers online. Positive feedback from other dropshippers can indicate a supplier's reliability and service quality.

5. Test Communication Responsiveness: Evaluate the responsiveness of suppliers when contacting them with inquiries. Prompt and helpful

communication is vital for smooth order processing and issue resolution.

6. Scrutinize Terms and Policies: Review supplier agreements, terms, and policies carefully. Pay attention to pricing, shipping fees, return policies, and any restrictions that might affect your dropshipping business.

7. Assess Order Fulfillment Efficiency: Inquire about the supplier's order fulfillment process and shipping times. Timely deliveries are crucial for maintaining customer satisfaction and building a reputable brand.

8. Request References: Ask potential suppliers for references from other dropshippers they work with. Talking to other dropshippers can provide valuable insights into the supplier's reliability and communication.

9. Evaluate Dropshipping Integrations: Check if the supplier has integrations with popular dropshipping platforms. An existing integration can streamline order processing and make inventory management more efficient.

10. Consider Geographical Proximity: Opt for suppliers located closer to your target market to potentially reduce shipping times and costs. However, prioritize reliability and product quality over proximity if needed.

11. Test with Small Orders: Start with small test orders to assess the supplier's performance and customer service. Gradually increase the order size once you are confident in their capabilities.

*Remember that building a strong relationship with your suppliers is essential for long-term success. Prioritize open communication, set clear expectations, and establish mutual trust. By diligently vetting suppliers and building reliable partnerships, you can ensure a positive dropshipping experience for your customers and foster growth for your business.*

# Evaluating Product Quality And Pricing

Evaluating product quality and pricing for your dropshipping business requires a balanced and thorough approach. Here's an original guide to help you make informed decisions:

1. Request Product Samples: Whenever possible, request product samples from potential suppliers before committing to a partnership. This hands-on evaluation allows you to assess the quality, design, and overall appeal of the products you will be selling.

2. Read Customer Reviews: Research customer reviews and feedback for the products you are considering. Genuine customer experiences can reveal insights into product quality, performance, and potential issues.

3. Compare Multiple Suppliers: Contact multiple suppliers for the same or similar products to compare pricing, product quality, and shipping options. This comparison will help you identify the most competitive and reliable options.

4. Analyze Pricing Structure: Understand the pricing structure of each supplier, including product costs, shipping fees, and any additional charges. Evaluate the overall cost to ensure profitability while maintaining competitive pricing for your customers.

5. Consider Product Specifications: Assess the specifications and features of the products. Look for detailed information regarding materials used, dimensions, and any certifications or standards the products adhere to.

6. Test Customer Support: Reach out to suppliers' customer support with inquiries or concerns. Quick and helpful responses indicate good customer service, which will be essential in case of any issues with product quality or fulfillment.

7. Check Return Policies: Review the return policies of suppliers in case customers request refunds or replacements. Understanding return procedures and costs will prepare you for handling potential returns.

8. Gauge Delivery Times: Inquire about estimated delivery times for different regions. Prompt shipping is vital for ensuring customer satisfaction and repeat business.

9. Seek Supplier Feedback: Ask other dropshippers or entrepreneurs about their experiences with specific suppliers. Feedback from fellow business owners can offer valuable insights into product quality and reliability.

10. Look for Brand Reputation: Consider the reputation of the brands or manufacturers associated with the products. Well-established and respected brands can instill confidence in your customers.

11. Consider Long-Term Viability: Evaluate the long-term viability of the products in your niche. Select products with enduring demand to ensure consistent sales over time.

*By meticulously evaluating product quality and pricing through hands-on testing, customer feedback, and supplier research, you can make well-informed decisions for your dropshipping business. Prioritize customer satisfaction, reliable suppliers, and competitive pricing to build a brand known for offering high-quality products and exceptional value in the market.*

# Ensuring Efficient Order Fulfillment

Ensuring efficient order fulfillment is vital for the success of your dropshipping business. Here's an original guide to help you streamline the process:

1. Reliable Supplier Partnerships: Establish strong relationships with reliable suppliers. Work with those who consistently meet shipping deadlines and maintain a high level of product quality. Open communication with suppliers is essential for smooth order processing.

2. Real-Time Inventory Management: Utilize inventory management tools that sync in real-time with your suppliers. This ensures that you have accurate stock levels, minimizing the risk of overselling and backorders.

3. Automation and Integration: Implement automation tools and integrate them with your e-commerce platform. Automated order processing, tracking, and notifications will save time and reduce the likelihood of errors.

4. Clear Product Availability Information: Display accurate product availability information on your online store. Inform customers upfront if a product is out of stock or has longer shipping times, managing their expectations proactively.

5. Fast Shipping Options: Offer expedited shipping options for customers who desire quicker delivery. Partner with suppliers who can fulfill such orders promptly to cater to different customer preferences.

6. Streamlined Order Processing: Streamline the order fulfillment process from the moment a customer places an order to shipment tracking. Reducing manual steps and delays will lead to more efficient order processing.

7. Monitor Order Status: Regularly monitor the status of orders with suppliers to ensure smooth processing and timely fulfillment. Address any issues promptly to prevent delays.

8. Clear Return and Refund Policies: Establish clear return and refund policies to handle customer inquiries effectively. Simplifying the return process will enhance customer satisfaction and loyalty.

9. Prioritize Customer Support: Provide excellent customer support to address any inquiries or concerns promptly. Keeping customers informed and engaged throughout the fulfillment process will build trust.

10. Test the Process: Regularly test the order fulfillment process from the customer's perspective. Identify potential pain points and make improvements to optimize the customer experience.

11. Plan for Peak Seasons: Prepare for peak seasons or holidays by increasing communication with suppliers and adjusting inventory levels accordingly. Anticipating high demand will prevent fulfillment bottlenecks.

*By focusing on reliable suppliers, automation, and customer-centric strategies, you can ensure efficient order fulfillment for your dropshipping business. Remember that a well-executed order fulfillment process not only leads to satisfied customers but also contributes to a positive brand reputation and steady business growth.*

* * *

# CHAPTER 5: CRAFTING EFFECTIVE PRODUCT LISTINGS

## Writing Compelling Product Descriptions

Writing compelling product descriptions is essential for capturing the attention of potential customers and driving sales on your dropshipping website. Here's an original guide to help you craft persuasive and engaging product descriptions:

1. Know Your Target Audience: Understand your target audience's needs, preferences, and pain points. Tailor your product descriptions to speak directly to their desires and showcase how the product meets their specific requirements.

2. Highlight Benefits, Not Just Features: Focus on the benefits that the product offers rather than merely listing its features. Explain how the product solves a problem or enhances the customer's life, making it more compelling and relevant.

3. Use Descriptive Language: Utilize descriptive language that paints a vivid picture in the customer's mind. Appeal to their senses, emotions, and imagination to create an immersive experience.

4. Create a Story: Tell a story around the product, engaging customers with narratives that evoke emotions and establish a connection. Stories help customers visualize themselves using the product, increasing the likelihood of a purchase.

5. Keep it Concise and Clear: While being descriptive, keep your product descriptions concise and easy to read. Avoid long paragraphs and use bullet points or short sentences to convey information effectively.

6. Incorporate Keywords: Integrate relevant keywords into your product descriptions to improve search engine visibility. Strive for a natural and seamless incorporation of keywords to maintain readability.

7. Address Objections: Anticipate and address potential customer objections in your product descriptions. Providing solutions to common concerns builds trust and confidence in your product.

8. Include Social Proof: Mention positive customer reviews, ratings, or testimonials to reinforce the product's quality and credibility. Social proof adds legitimacy and encourages customers to make a purchase.

9. Create a Sense of Urgency: Use persuasive language to create a sense of urgency and encourage customers to act quickly. Limited-time offers or scarcity of stock can motivate them to make a decision.

10. Offer Personalization: Where applicable, offer personalization options for products. Mentioning the ability to customize products according to customers' preferences enhances the sense of exclusivity and uniqueness.

11. End with a Clear Call-to-Action: Conclude your product descriptions with a clear and compelling call-to-action. Encourage customers to add the product to their cart, complete the purchase, or explore related items.

*By crafting product descriptions that speak directly to your audience, evoke emotions, and emphasize benefits, you can entice customers to engage with your dropshipping website and make confident purchasing decisions. Remember that writing compelling product descriptions is an art that combines creativity, empathy, and a deep understanding of your customers' needs.*

# Capturing High-Quality Product Images

Capturing high-quality product images is essential for presenting your dropshipping products in the best light and enticing customers to make a purchase. Here's an original guide to help you achieve professional product images:

1. Invest in Lighting: Use natural light or invest in lighting equipment to achieve well-lit product images. Soft, diffused light reduces harsh shadows and enhances product details, resulting in appealing visuals.

2. Use a Tripod: Stabilize your camera or smartphone with a tripod to eliminate blurriness and ensure sharp, clear images. This steadiness allows you to capture professional-looking photos consistently.

3. Choose the Right Background: Opt for a clean and uncluttered background that highlights the product without distractions. Solid-colored backgrounds or lightbox setups can create a professional and consistent look.

4. Focus on Composition: Pay attention to product composition and framing. Place the product at the center or following the rule of thirds to create balanced and visually pleasing images.

5. Capture Multiple Angles: Photograph the product from various angles to showcase its features comprehensively. Front, back, side, and close-up shots provide customers with a complete view of the product.

6. Highlight Unique Features: Emphasize the product's unique features and intricate details. Close-up shots allow customers to appreciate the craftsmanship and quality of the item.

7. Use Props Wisely: Consider using props that complement the product and help convey its usage or scale. However, ensure that the props do not overshadow the main item.

8. Show Products in Use: Demonstrate how the product is used in real-life situations. Lifestyle images can help customers envision themselves using the product, enhancing its appeal.

9. Optimize Image Size: Resize and optimize your images for web use to maintain high-quality visuals while ensuring fast page loading times on your dropshipping website.

10. Edit and Enhance: Post-process your images to adjust brightness, contrast, and color balance. Light editing can enhance the overall aesthetics without misrepresenting the product.

11. Consistency is Key: Maintain a consistent style and size for all product images to create a cohesive and professional-looking product catalog.

*Remember that high-quality product images are an integral part of your dropshipping website's visual appeal. They act as a gateway to capturing customer attention and inspiring confidence in your products. By dedicating time and effort to capture and present products in the best possible light, you'll create a visually engaging and trustworthy online store for your dropshipping business.*

# Optimizing Product Titles And Metadata For Search Engines

Finding high-quality product images for your dropshipping website can be achieved through several reliable sources. Here's an original guide to help you locate visually appealing images:

1. Supplier Catalogs: Many dropshipping suppliers provide professional product images as part of their catalogs. Reach out to your suppliers and inquire about image assets that you can use for your website.

2. Manufacturer Websites: Visit the official websites of manufacturers whose products you plan to dropship. Often, manufacturers offer product images that can be used by authorized sellers.

3. Stock Photo Websites: Explore reputable stock photo websites like Shutterstock, Adobe Stock, or Unsplash. These platforms offer a vast selection of high-quality images that you can purchase or use under Creative Commons licenses.

4. Product Review Sites: Browse product review websites and blogs related to your niche. They often feature product images that you can use, as long as you attribute the source properly.

5. Social Media: Search for product images on social media platforms, especially Instagram and Pinterest. Many brands and influencers share visually appealing images that can be a great fit for your dropshipping website.

6. Collaborate with Influencers: Collaborate with influencers or content creators within your niche. They may provide you with high-quality images featuring your dropshipping products in real-life settings.

7. DIY Photography: If you have the products in hand, consider taking your own product photos. Invest in a decent camera or use a smartphone with a good camera and practice your photography skills to capture unique and personalized images.

8. Online Marketplaces: Check e-commerce marketplaces like Amazon or eBay, where sellers often upload product images that you can use as references or with permission.

9. Subscription Services: Some online platforms offer subscription-based services that provide access to a wide range of product images. Consider joining such services if they align with your budget and requirements.

10. Request Supplier Collaboration: Reach out to your suppliers and request permission to use their product images for your website. Building a good relationship with your suppliers may open doors for image-sharing opportunities.

*Always ensure that you have the right to use the images you find, either by purchasing them, obtaining permission, or using images with appropriate licenses. Additionally, maintain consistency in image styles to create a visually appealing and cohesive dropshipping website that leaves a positive impression on your customers.*

* * *

# CHAPTER 6: DRIVING TRAFFIC AND CONVERSIONS

## Exploring Various Marketing Channels

Optimizing product titles and metadata is essential for improving your dropshipping website's search engine visibility and attracting organic traffic. Here's an original guide to help you effectively optimize these elements:

1. Keyword Research: Conduct thorough keyword research to identify relevant and high-traffic search terms related to your products. Use keyword research tools to discover popular phrases that potential customers use when searching for products in your niche.

2. Concise and Descriptive Titles: Craft product titles that are concise, descriptive, and include primary keywords. Highlight the main features, benefits, and unique selling points of the product within the title.

3. Avoid Keyword Stuffing: While incorporating keywords is essential, avoid keyword stuffing (excessive and unnatural use of keywords) in your titles and metadata. Focus on creating natural-sounding content that provides value to your audience.

4. Unique Meta Descriptions: Write unique and compelling meta descriptions for each product page. Meta descriptions serve as a brief summary of the product, encouraging users to click through to your website from search engine results.

5. Include Product Attributes: Integrate essential product attributes in your titles and metadata, such as brand name, color, size, and other relevant specifications. This specificity helps customers find the exact product they're looking for.

6. Localize when Applicable: If you target a specific location or region, consider adding localized keywords to your titles and metadata. Local optimization can improve visibility in regional search results.

7. Utilize Structured Data Markup: Implement structured data markup (e.g., schema.org) to provide search engines with additional information about your products. This can enhance how your products are displayed in search results, increasing click-through rates.

8. Prioritize Mobile Optimization: Ensure that your product titles and metadata are optimized for mobile devices. With the increasing use of smartphones for online searches, mobile-friendly content is crucial for ranking well on search engines.

9. Regularly Update and Optimize: Stay up-to-date with changes in keyword trends and search algorithms. Regularly review and optimize your product titles and metadata to align with the latest search engine best practices.

10. Test and Analyze: Experiment with different title formats and metadata to see which ones yield the best results. Use analytics tools to track user engagement and conversions to gauge the effectiveness of your optimization efforts.

*By implementing these original strategies, you can optimize product titles and metadata effectively, increasing your dropshipping website's visibility in search engine results. Appearing prominently in relevant searches will drive more organic traffic to your website and boost your chances of attracting potential customers to explore and purchase from your product offerings.*

# Implementing Social Media Strategies

Exploring various marketing channels is crucial to reach a broader audience and drive traffic to your dropshipping website. Here's an original guide to help you effectively explore these channels:

1. Research Your Target Audience: Start by understanding your target audience's preferences, behavior, and online habits. This insight will guide you in selecting the most relevant marketing channels to reach and engage them effectively.

2. Begin with Content Marketing: Create valuable and informative content related to your niche. Start a blog, produce engaging videos, or share useful guides. Content marketing establishes your authority and attracts organic traffic over time.

3. Harness Social Media: Leverage popular social media platforms that align with your target audience. Create engaging posts, share product images, and interact with your followers regularly. Social media allows you to build a community and generate brand awareness.

4. Explore Influencer Marketing: Collaborate with influencers or micro-influencers in your niche. Partnering with influential personalities can

significantly expand your reach and credibility among their followers.
5. Utilize Email Marketing: Build an email list and engage subscribers with personalized offers, product updates, and valuable content. Email marketing is a cost-effective way to nurture leads and foster customer loyalty.

6. Experiment with Pay-Per-Click (PPC) Advertising: Start with PPC advertising on platforms like Google Ads or social media. Set a budget and monitor the performance of your ads to optimize for maximum ROI.

7. Tap into Affiliate Marketing: Implement an affiliate program to encourage others to promote your products. Affiliates earn commissions for driving sales, allowing you to reach audiences beyond your immediate reach.

8. Host Webinars and Live Events: Conduct webinars or live events to showcase your products and engage directly with potential customers. Webinars provide an interactive platform to answer questions and build relationships.

9. Collaborate with Complementary Brands: Partner with other businesses in your niche to cross-promote products. This strategic collaboration can lead to shared audiences and increased brand exposure.

10. Analyze and Adjust: Continuously monitor the performance of your marketing efforts. Use analytics to track conversion rates, click-through rates, and customer engagement. Adjust your strategies based on data-driven insights.

11. Stay Updated with Trends: Stay abreast of the latest marketing trends and emerging platforms. Be open to experimenting with new channels and tactics to stay ahead of the competition.

By adopting a diversified approach to marketing, you can explore various channels that align with your target audience and product offerings. Emphasizing authentic engagement and providing value to your audience will foster a strong brand presence and drive sustained growth for your dropshipping website.

# Harnessing The Power Of SEO And Content Marketing

Harnessing the power of SEO (Search Engine Optimization) and content marketing can significantly elevate your dropshipping website's online visibility, attract organic traffic, and boost conversions. Here's an original guide to effectively utilize these strategies:

1. Keyword Research: Conduct thorough keyword research to identify relevant search terms used by your target audience. Integrate these keywords strategically into your website content to improve its search engine ranking.

2. Create High-Quality Content: Develop valuable and informative content that addresses your audience's needs and interests. This can include product guides, tutorials, blog posts, and engaging videos that showcase your expertise and build trust with potential customers.

3. Optimize On-Page SEO: Optimize your website's meta titles, meta descriptions, headers, and URLs with relevant keywords. Focus on crafting compelling and click-worthy meta tags that entice users to click through from search engine results.

4. Implement Internal Linking: Utilize internal linking to connect related content on your website. This improves website navigation, user experience, and helps search engines understand the structure and relevance of your content.

5. Mobile-Friendly Design: Ensure that your dropshipping website is fully optimized for mobile devices. Mobile-friendly sites rank higher in mobile search results and cater to the growing number of mobile users.

6. User-Generated Content: Encourage user-generated content such as product reviews, testimonials, and customer stories. User-generated content not only adds credibility but also provides additional keyword-rich content for search engines.

7. Guest Blogging and Backlinks: Contribute guest posts to reputable websites within your niche. Guest blogging allows you to showcase your expertise, attract new audiences, and build valuable backlinks to your dropshipping website, boosting its authority.

8. Focus on Long-Tail Keywords: Target long-tail keywords (specific, multi-word phrases) in your content. These keywords often have less competition and can attract more qualified traffic with a higher chance of conversion.

9. Regularly Update Content: Keep your website's content fresh and up-to-date. Regularly update product descriptions, blog posts, and other pages to show search engines that your website provides valuable and current information.

10. Monitor Analytics: Track the performance of your content and SEO efforts using analytics tools. Analyze user behavior, traffic sources, and keyword rankings to identify areas for improvement and refine your strategies.

11. Be Patient and Consistent: SEO and content marketing require time and consistency to yield significant results. Stay patient, and continue creating valuable content while following SEO best practices to build a strong online presence.

*By strategically combining SEO techniques and content marketing efforts, you can establish your dropshipping website as an authoritative source in your niche, attract organic traffic, and ultimately drive more conversions. The synergy of these strategies allows you to connect with your target audience, enhance your online visibility, and create lasting relationships with customers.*

*  *  *

# CHAPTER 7: CUSTOMER SERVICE AND RELATIONSHIP MANAGEMENT

## Establishing Exceptional Customer Service Standards

Establishing exceptional customer service standards is essential for building trust, fostering customer loyalty, and ensuring the success of your dropshipping website. Here's an original guide to help you create a remarkable customer service experience:

1. Set Clear Communication Channels: Provide multiple communication channels such as email, live chat, and phone support. Ensure that customers can easily reach you and receive timely responses to their inquiries.

2. Personalize Customer Interactions: Address customers by their names and use personalized greetings in communication. Show genuine interest in their needs and provide tailored assistance.

3. Fast and Transparent Responses: Respond to customer inquiries promptly and transparently. Keep customers informed about order status, shipping delays, and any potential issues, fostering trust and confidence.

4. Prioritize Problem Resolution: Resolve customer issues efficiently and professionally. Empower your customer service team to make decisions that benefit the customer, resolving problems on the first contact.

5. 24/7 Support: Offer round-the-clock customer support, even if it's through automated responses during off-hours. This ensures customers feel supported at any time of the day.

6. Educate and Empower Customers: Provide educational resources and guides to help customers make informed decisions. Empower them with the knowledge to choose the right products and use them effectively.

7. Hassle-Free Returns and Refunds: Implement a straightforward and customer-friendly return policy. Make the returns and refund process seamless, showing customers that their satisfaction is your priority.

8. Acknowledge Feedback: Welcome customer feedback, whether positive or negative. Acknowledge and appreciate positive feedback, and use constructive criticism to improve your services.

9. Surprise and Delight: Go the extra mile to surprise and delight customers. Include small thank-you notes, freebies, or personalized touches with their orders to create memorable experiences.

10. Proactive Communication: Anticipate customer needs and reach out proactively. For example, inform customers about product restocks or upcoming promotions they might be interested in.

11. Continuous Improvement: Regularly review and improve your customer service processes based on customer feedback and data. Embrace a culture of continuous improvement to deliver exceptional experiences.

*By prioritizing customer satisfaction, personalized interactions, and continuous improvement, you can establish exceptional customer service standards for your dropshipping website. A positive customer experience not only leads to repeat business but also encourages word-of-mouth referrals, helping your dropshipping business thrive in the competitive e-commerce landscape.*

# Dealing With Customer Inquiries And Complaints

Dealing with customer inquiries and complaints promptly and professionally is vital for maintaining a positive reputation and fostering customer loyalty on your dropshipping website. Here are some original ways to handle customer inquiries and complaints effectively:

1. Respond with Empathy: Approach every inquiry and complaint with empathy and understanding. Acknowledge the customer's concerns and show genuine care about resolving their issue.

2. Timely Responses: Respond to customer inquiries and complaints as quickly as possible. Prompt responses demonstrate that you value their time and prioritize their satisfaction.

3. Active Listening: Practice active listening when interacting with customers. Allow them to express their concerns fully without interruption, and ask clarifying questions to understand their needs better.

4. Stay Calm and Professional: Remain calm and composed, even in challenging situations. Maintain a professional tone and avoid taking complaints personally, focusing on finding solutions instead.

5. Offer Apologies and Solutions: Apologize for any inconvenience caused and provide clear solutions to resolve the issue. Tailor your responses to

meet the customer's specific needs and expectations.

6. Personalized Solutions: Whenever possible, offer personalized solutions that go beyond standard procedures. Addressing individual concerns uniquely can make customers feel valued and appreciated.

7. Escalate When Necessary: If a customer's issue requires further attention or approval from higher management, escalate it promptly while keeping the customer informed about the process.

8. Follow Up: After resolving an inquiry or complaint, follow up with the customer to ensure their satisfaction. This follow-up shows that you genuinely care about their experience.

9. Learn from Feedback: Treat complaints as opportunities for improvement. Analyze recurring issues and use customer feedback to identify areas where you can enhance your products or services.

10. Provide Compensation Thoughtfully: When appropriate, offer compensation such as discounts, vouchers, or free shipping as a gesture of goodwill. Thoughtful compensation can turn a negative experience into a positive one.

11. Keep Records: Maintain detailed records of customer inquiries and resolutions. This documentation helps track common issues, evaluate customer service performance, and ensure consistency in responses.

*By handling customer inquiries and complaints with care, responsiveness, and professionalism, you can turn dissatisfied customers into loyal advocates for your dropshipping website. Positive interactions and effective resolutions not only retain customers but also contribute to a strong brand reputation that attracts new customers through positive word-of-mouth referrals.*

# Building Long-Term Customer Relationships

Building long-term customer relationships is crucial for the sustained success of your dropshipping website. Here are some original ways to foster lasting connections with your customers:

1. Personalized Communication: Address customers by their names and use personalized greetings in emails and messages. Tailor your communication to their preferences and previous interactions, making them feel valued and understood.

2. Excellent Customer Service: Prioritize exceptional customer service at every touchpoint. Be responsive, helpful, and proactive in addressing their needs, inquiries, and concerns.

3. Loyalty Programs: Implement a loyalty program that rewards customers for repeat purchases and referrals. Offer exclusive discounts, special offers, or points-based rewards to encourage ongoing engagement.

4. Engaging Content: Create valuable and engaging content on your website, blog, and social media platforms. Share relevant tips, industry news, and educational content that resonates with your audience.

5. Surprise and Delight: Surprise customers with unexpected gestures, such as personalized thank-you notes, small gifts, or exclusive offers. These thoughtful acts can leave a lasting positive impression.

6. Feedback and Surveys: Seek regular feedback from customers through surveys and reviews. Act on their suggestions and demonstrate that their opinions matter in shaping your business.

7. Follow Up: Follow up with customers after purchases to ensure their satisfaction and inquire about their overall experience. This follow-up shows that you care about their well-being beyond the transaction.

8. Transparent Policies: Maintain clear and transparent policies regarding shipping, returns, and refunds. Honesty and reliability foster trust, which is vital for building lasting relationships.

9. Celebrate Milestones: Celebrate special occasions, such as customer birthdays or anniversary milestones with your brand. Send personalized messages or offer exclusive promotions to commemorate these moments.

10. Social Media Engagement: Engage with customers on social media platforms. Respond to comments, mentions, and direct messages promptly, fostering a sense of community and connection.

11. Support Social Causes: Engage in social initiatives or support causes that align with your brand values. Demonstrate social responsibility to resonate with customers who share similar beliefs.

*By prioritizing personalized communication, exceptional service, and meaningful gestures, you can cultivate long-term relationships with your customers. Building trust, loyalty, and emotional connections will not only encourage repeat business but also turn customers into brand advocates who refer your dropshipping website to others.*

* * *

# CHAPTER 8: MANAGING OPERATIONS AND SCALING UP

## Streamlining Order Fulfillment And Logistics

Streamlining order fulfillment and logistics is essential for efficient and smooth operations on your dropshipping website. Here are some original ways to achieve this:

1. Establish Reliable Supplier Partnerships: Work closely with reputable and dependable suppliers. Choose suppliers who have a track record of timely order processing and accurate fulfillment.

2. Real-Time Inventory Management: Implement inventory management systems that sync in real-time with your suppliers. This ensures you have accurate stock information, reducing the risk of overselling or backorders.

3. Automate Order Processing: Utilize automation tools to streamline order processing, from customer checkout to supplier communication. Automated systems can handle repetitive tasks, saving time and minimizing errors.

4. Optimize Packaging and Shipping: Standardize packaging processes to ensure consistency and efficiency. Explore shipping options to find the most cost-effective and reliable carriers for your products.

5. Offer Tracking and Notifications: Provide customers with tracking information once orders are shipped. Proactively communicate any delays or updates to keep customers informed.

6. Consolidate Shipments: If possible, consolidate multiple orders going to the same location. This reduces shipping costs and enhances the overall efficiency of order fulfillment.

7. Implement a Returns Management System: Establish a clear and user-friendly returns management system. Make it easy for customers to request returns and track the status of their returns.

8. Monitor Key Performance Indicators (KPIs): Track KPIs related to order fulfillment, such as order processing time, shipping time, and customer satisfaction. Regularly analyze data to identify areas for improvement.

9. Offer Expedited Shipping Options: Consider offering expedited shipping for customers who require faster delivery. Partner with suppliers who can fulfill these orders promptly.

10. Continuous Improvement: Continuously assess and optimize your fulfillment and logistics processes. Solicit feedback from customers and suppliers to identify areas for improvement.

11. Customer Support Integration: Integrate customer support with order fulfillment processes. Enable customer support agents to access order information quickly to resolve inquiries effectively.

*By streamlining order fulfillment and logistics, you can create a seamless and satisfying shopping experience for your customers. Efficient operations not only lead to increased customer satisfaction but also contribute to a positive brand reputation, driving customer loyalty and repeat business for your dropshipping website.*

# Automating Repetitive Tasks

Automating repetitive tasks is a smart way to save time, increase efficiency, and scale your dropshipping website. Here's an original guide to help you automate tasks effectively:

1. Utilize E-commerce Platforms: Choose a robust e-commerce platform that offers automation features. Many platforms provide tools for order processing, inventory management, and customer communication.

2. Implement Chatbots: Integrate AI-powered chatbots to handle customer inquiries and provide instant responses 24/7. Chatbots can answer common questions and redirect more complex queries to human support when needed.

3. Automate Email Marketing: Utilize email marketing automation tools to send personalized emails, welcome sequences, and follow-up messages based on customer behavior and triggers.

4. Set Up Auto-Order Processing: Enable auto-order processing with your suppliers. When customers place orders on your website, the system automatically sends purchase details to the supplier for fulfillment.
5. Use Social Media Schedulers: Schedule and automate your social media posts using scheduling tools. Plan your content in advance and have it automatically published on your chosen platforms.

6. Implement CRM Systems: Utilize Customer Relationship Management (CRM) software to automate customer data management, segment audiences, and track interactions.

7. Auto-Generate Invoices: Set up an automated system to generate and send invoices to customers after each purchase. This saves time and ensures consistency in invoicing procedures.

8. Integrate Shipping Software: Use shipping software that integrates with your e-commerce platform and suppliers. This streamlines the process of generating shipping labels and tracking orders.

9. Enable Abandoned Cart Recovery: Implement abandoned cart recovery emails to automatically remind customers about their incomplete purchases and encourage them to complete the checkout process.

10. Sync Inventory Management: Ensure that your inventory management system syncs in real-time with your suppliers. This prevents overselling and helps maintain accurate stock levels.

11. Track and Analyze: Continuously track the performance of your automated processes and analyze data to identify areas for improvement. Use analytics to optimize and fine-tune your automation strategies.

*By leveraging automation tools and technologies, you can free up time to focus on strategic decision-making, customer engagement, and business growth. Automation not only enhances productivity but also enhances the overall customer experience, leading to greater satisfaction and loyalty for your dropshipping website.*

# Strategies For Scaling Your Dropshipping Business

Scaling your dropshipping business requires careful planning, strategic decisions, and a focus on sustainable growth. Here are some original strategies to help you effectively scale your dropshipping business:

1. Diversify Product Offerings: Expand your product catalog to cater to a broader audience. Introduce complementary products and explore new niches to increase the variety of offerings.

2. Collaborate with More Suppliers: Partner with multiple reliable suppliers to access a wider range of products and ensure a steady supply chain. This minimizes the risk of relying heavily on a single supplier.

3. Optimize Operations: Streamline and automate key processes such as order fulfillment, inventory management, and customer support. Efficiency and scalability go hand in hand.

4. Invest in Marketing: Allocate resources to various marketing channels, including social media, content marketing, SEO, and paid advertising. This boosts brand visibility and attracts a larger audience.

5. Focus on Customer Retention: Prioritize customer satisfaction and loyalty. Implement loyalty programs, personalized communication, and excellent customer service to retain existing customers and encourage repeat purchases.

6. Expand Target Markets: Identify new geographical markets and demographics to target. Tailor your marketing efforts to appeal to diverse audiences.

7. Offer Exclusive Deals: Create time-limited promotions, flash sales, and exclusive discounts to incentivize customer purchases and create a sense of urgency.

8. Build a Strong Brand Identity: Invest in branding to create a distinct and memorable identity for your dropshipping business. A strong brand presence fosters trust and recognition among customers.

9. Monitor Metrics: Regularly track and analyze key performance indicators (KPIs) such as conversion rates, average order value, and customer acquisition cost. Use data-driven insights to inform your scaling decisions.

10. Invest in Customer Acquisition: Allocate resources to acquire new customers through targeted marketing efforts and lead generation strategies.

11. Secure Reliable Payment and Shipping Providers: Partner with reputable payment processors and shipping providers to ensure smooth transactions and timely deliveries, instilling confidence in your customers.

*Remember that scaling a dropshipping business should be a gradual and well-planned process. Focus on maintaining quality, providing exceptional customer experiences, and staying adaptable to market trends and customer preferences. Scaling successfully ensures sustainable growth and positions your dropshipping business for long-term success in the competitive e-commerce landscape.*

* * *

# CHAPTER 9: ANALYTICS AND OPTIMIZATION

## Leveraging Data To Make Informed Decisions

Leveraging data effectively can be a game-changer for your dropshipping website, enabling you to make informed decisions that drive growth and success. Here are some original ways to harness data:

1. Data-Driven Analytics: Utilize web analytics tools to track and analyze user behavior, traffic sources, and conversion rates on your website. Insights from these analytics help identify strengths, weaknesses, and opportunities for improvement.

2. Customer Segmentation: Segment your customer data based on demographics, purchase history, and behavior. This segmentation enables you to personalize marketing efforts and tailor product recommendations to specific customer groups.]

3. A/B Testing: Conduct A/B tests on various elements of your website, such as product images, call-to-action buttons, or pricing strategies. Analyze the results to identify which variations perform better and optimize accordingly.

4. Inventory Management: Use data to optimize inventory levels and avoid overstocking or stockouts. Historical sales data can help predict demand patterns, allowing you to maintain adequate stock levels without tying up excess capital.

5. Customer Feedback: Collect and analyze customer feedback through surveys, reviews, and social media interactions. Customer insights provide valuable feedback to improve products, services, and overall customer experience.

6. Competitive Analysis: Gather data on your competitors' strategies, pricing, and promotions. This information helps you identify your competitive edge and adapt your dropshipping approach accordingly.

7. Customer Lifetime Value (CLV): Calculate the CLV of your customers based on their past purchase behavior. This metric helps you prioritize high-value customers and tailor retention efforts.

8. Email Marketing Insights: Use email marketing data to track open rates, click-through rates, and conversion rates for various email campaigns. Optimize your email marketing strategy based on data-driven insights.

9. Real-Time Sales Monitoring: Monitor sales in real-time to stay agile and respond promptly to changes in demand or market trends.

10. Website Heatmaps: Utilize heatmaps to visualize user behavior on your website, revealing popular areas and potential pain points. Use this data to enhance website design and optimize the user experience.

11. Forecasting and Planning: Use historical data and market trends to forecast future demand and plan your marketing and inventory strategies accordingly.

*By incorporating data-driven decision-making into your dropshipping operations, you gain a competitive advantage and the ability to pivot effectively in response to market changes. Data empowers you to identify growth opportunities, optimize marketing efforts, and tailor your dropshipping approach to meet the evolving needs of your customers.*

# Tracking Key Performance Indicators

Tracking key performance indicators (KPIs) is crucial for monitoring the success and growth of your dropshipping website. Here's a reasonable guide to help you effectively track KPIs:

1. Define Your KPIs: Start by identifying the KPIs that align with your dropshipping business goals. Common KPIs include conversion rate, average order value, customer acquisition cost, and customer retention rate.

2. Set Benchmarks: Establish benchmarks or targets for each KPI based on industry standards, historical data, or desired performance levels. These benchmarks serve as reference points for assessing progress.

3. Utilize Web Analytics: Implement web analytics tools like Google Analytics to track website traffic, user behavior, and conversions. Analyze data regularly to gain insights into customer journeys and website performance.

4. Monitor Sales Metrics: Track sales data, including revenue, profit margins, and individual product performance. This data helps identify high-performing products and areas for improvement.

5. Measure Customer Satisfaction: Collect customer feedback through surveys, reviews, and social media interactions. Monitoring customer satisfaction helps gauge the effectiveness of your customer service and overall shopping experience.

6. Analyze Marketing Campaigns: Measure the performance of your marketing efforts, such as email campaigns, social media ads, and SEO strategies. Analyze click-through rates, conversion rates, and return on investment (ROI).

7. Assess Inventory Management: Monitor inventory turnover rates, stock levels, and order fulfillment time. Efficient inventory management ensures product availability while minimizing carrying costs.

8. Review Shipping and Delivery Metrics: Track shipping times, delivery success rates, and return rates. Reliable and timely shipping is crucial for customer satisfaction.

9. Calculate Customer Lifetime Value: Analyze the customer lifetime value (CLV) to understand the long-term profitability of your customer base. A higher CLV indicates better customer retention and loyalty.
10. Use Visualizations: Present KPI data in visual formats such as charts and graphs to facilitate easy understanding and comparisons over time.

11. Regularly Review and Adjust: Regularly review KPI data to spot trends, identify opportunities, and address performance gaps. Use this data to make informed decisions and adjust your dropshipping strategies accordingly.

*By consistently tracking KPIs, you gain valuable insights into your dropshipping website's performance, enabling you to make data-driven decisions that optimize operations, drive growth, and enhance customer satisfaction. Remember to revisit and update your KPIs periodically as your business evolves to stay relevant and focused on the metrics that matter most.*

# Implementing Continuous Improvement Strategies

Implementing continuous improvement strategies is essential for ensuring your dropshipping website remains competitive and optimized for success. Here are some original ways to foster a culture of continuous improvement:

1. Regular Performance Reviews: Conduct regular performance reviews of your website, analyzing key metrics, customer feedback, and user behavior. Use this data to identify areas for enhancement and make data-driven decisions.
2. A/B Testing: Continuously run A/B tests on various website elements, such as product images, headlines, or call-to-action buttons. Compare results to find the most effective variations and optimize user engagement.

3. Customer Feedback Loop: Create a customer feedback loop, actively soliciting feedback through surveys, reviews, and social media interactions. Use this feedback to make iterative improvements based on customer preferences and needs.

4. Empower Your Team: Encourage your team to contribute ideas and suggestions for improvement. Emphasize open communication and value team members' insights into enhancing processes and customer experiences.

5. Monitor Industry Trends: Stay up-to-date with the latest industry trends and best practices in dropshipping. Adopt innovative strategies and technologies to stay ahead of the competition.

6. Set Improvement Goals: Define specific improvement goals for your dropshipping website. Regularly assess progress towards these goals and adjust strategies as needed to achieve desired outcomes.

7. Competitive Analysis: Conduct regular competitive analysis to benchmark your performance against industry leaders. Learn from successful competitors and apply relevant insights to enhance your website's offerings.
8. Embrace Innovation: Embrace innovation and experimentation in your dropshipping approach. Be open to trying new ideas and technologies that can optimize operations and enhance the customer experience.

9. Collaborate with Suppliers: Engage in continuous improvement discussions with your suppliers. Collaborate to optimize order fulfillment, shipping processes, and product quality.

10. Measure Customer Satisfaction: Continuously monitor customer satisfaction metrics, such as Net Promoter Score (NPS) and customer retention rates. Address any issues promptly to enhance customer loyalty.

11. Data-Driven Decision-Making: Base decisions on data rather than assumptions. Leverage analytics and customer insights to guide improvement initiatives and validate the impact of changes.

*By fostering a culture of continuous improvement, your dropshipping website can adapt to evolving market demands, enhance customer satisfaction, and achieve sustained growth. Regularly review performance, engage with customers and suppliers, and embrace innovative strategies to ensure your website remains a dynamic and thriving business in the competitive e-commerce landscape.*

* * *

# CHAPTER 10: OVERCOMING CHALLENGES AND PITFALLS

## Dealing With Competition And Saturation

Dealing with competition and saturation in the dropshipping industry requires a strategic approach to differentiate your website and stand out from the crowd. Here are some original ways to tackle these challenges:

1. Niche Selection: Identify a unique and specialized niche within your industry. Focusing on a specific niche allows you to target a more defined audience and become an expert in that area.

2. Unique Value Proposition: Clearly define your unique value proposition. Highlight what sets your dropshipping website apart from competitors, whether it's exceptional customer service, exclusive products, or faster shipping times.

3. Quality Product Curation: Curate high-quality products from trusted suppliers. Emphasize product quality, authenticity, and value to build trust and credibility among your customers.

4. Customer-Centric Approach: Prioritize excellent customer experiences. Provide personalized support, engage with customers on social media, and actively seek feedback to continuously improve your services.

5. Exclusive Product Bundles: Create exclusive product bundles or packages that offer additional value to customers. These bundles can entice customers to choose your website over competitors.

6. Expand Marketing Channels: Diversify your marketing efforts across various channels, such as social media, content marketing, influencer collaborations, and email marketing. Reach a broader audience to increase brand visibility.

7. Competitive Pricing: Offer competitive pricing without compromising on product quality or customer service. Regularly review pricing strategies to stay competitive in the market.

8. Focus on Branding: Invest in building a strong brand identity. Create a consistent brand image through logo, color scheme, and messaging that resonates with your target audience.

9. Monitor and Adapt: Keep a close eye on market trends, customer preferences, and competitor strategies. Be prepared to adapt your approach as needed to stay relevant and meet changing demands.

10. Loyalty and Rewards: Implement a loyalty program to incentivize repeat purchases and customer referrals. Offer rewards and exclusive perks to encourage customer loyalty.

11. Continuous Improvement: Embrace continuous improvement as a core value in your business. Regularly assess your performance, learn from competitors, and strive to be at the forefront of innovation.

*By adopting these original strategies, you can navigate competition and saturation in the dropshipping industry effectively. A combination of differentiation, customer-centricity, and a commitment to continuous improvement will position your dropshipping website for long-term success and sustained growth amidst the challenges of a competitive market.*

# Mitigating Risks And Handling Unforeseen Circumstances

Mitigating risks and handling unforeseen circumstances is crucial for safeguarding your dropshipping website's operations and maintaining resilience. Here are some original ways to achieve this:

1. Diversify Supplier Partnerships: Work with multiple reliable suppliers to reduce dependency on a single source. Diversification minimizes the impact of potential supplier issues, such as stock shortages or shipping delays.

2. Maintain Safety Stock: Keep safety stock of essential products to handle unexpected spikes in demand or delays from suppliers. Safety stock provides a buffer and ensures continuity in fulfilling customer orders.

3. Monitor Inventory Regularly: Implement real-time inventory monitoring to stay informed about stock levels. This allows you to proactively address any inventory issues before they escalate.

4. Contingency Planning: Develop contingency plans for various scenarios, such as supplier disruptions, shipping delays, or changes in market conditions. Having predefined plans helps you respond swiftly to unforeseen events.

5. Insure Your Business: Consider business insurance that covers potential risks like product liability, shipping losses, or other operational disruptions.

6. Customer Communication: Communicate transparently with customers about any potential delays or issues. Proactively inform them about the status of their orders to manage expectations.

7. Establish Strong Customer Service: Prioritize exceptional customer service, especially during challenging times. Promptly address customer inquiries and concerns to maintain their trust.

8. Monitor Market Trends: Stay informed about industry trends and changes in consumer behavior. Being aware of market shifts allows you to adapt your strategies proactively.

9. Monitor Financial Health: Regularly assess your financial health to ensure you have adequate reserves to handle unforeseen circumstances.

10. Monitor Key Performance Indicators (KPIs): Keep track of important KPIs like conversion rates, average order value, and customer retention. Monitoring these metrics helps you identify early warning signs and respond accordingly.

11. Collaborate with Industry Peers: Connect with other dropshippers or e-commerce entrepreneurs to share insights and experiences. Learning from others can help you anticipate potential risks and handle them effectively.

*By incorporating these original strategies into your dropshipping business, you can minimize risks and navigate unforeseen circumstances with confidence. Proactive planning, strong communication, and the ability to adapt to changing situations are key to maintaining stability and success in the dynamic world of dropshipping.*

# Nurturing Resilience And Adapting To Change

Nurturing resilience and embracing adaptability are essential traits for success in the ever-evolving dropshipping industry. Here's an original guide to help you foster resilience and adaptability for your dropshipping website:

1. Cultivate a Growth Mindset: Adopt a growth mindset that embraces challenges as opportunities for learning and improvement. Embrace change as a catalyst for innovation and development.

2. Stay Informed: Stay up-to-date with industry trends, market dynamics, and emerging technologies. Being well-informed empowers you to anticipate changes and make informed decisions.

3. Proactive Planning: Develop contingency plans for potential challenges and disruptions. Proactively address risks and have predefined strategies to handle unexpected circumstances.

4. Monitor Customer Feedback: Listen to customer feedback and adapt based on their needs and preferences. Customer insights can guide you in refining your offerings and customer experience.

5. Embrace Flexibility: Be open to trying new strategies and approaches. Embrace flexibility in your business model to adapt swiftly to changing market demands.

6. Collaborate and Network: Engage with other industry professionals, attend conferences, and participate in networking events. Collaborating with peers allows you to gain insights and support from others facing similar challenges.

7. Test and Iterate: Embrace a culture of experimentation and continuous improvement. Test new ideas, analyze results, and iterate based on data-driven insights.

8. Build a Resilient Team: Surround yourself with a resilient team that embraces challenges and is motivated to overcome obstacles. Foster a positive work environment that encourages innovation and creativity.

9. Develop Long-Term Strategies: Balance short-term tactics with long-term vision. Develop sustainable strategies that can adapt to evolving market conditions.

10. Celebrate Successes: Acknowledge and celebrate milestones and successes, no matter how small. Positive reinforcement boosts morale and motivates your team to tackle future challenges.

11. Reflect and Learn: Regularly assess your experiences, both successes, and setbacks. Learn from past events and use those lessons to strengthen your resilience and adaptability.

*By nurturing resilience and embracing adaptability, you position your dropshipping website for longevity and growth. These qualities empower you to navigate uncertainties, embrace change, and turn challenges into opportunities for innovation and improvement. A resilient and adaptable approach ensures your dropshipping business can withstand the dynamic e-commerce landscape and thrive in the face of change.*

**Conclusion:**

"Start Selling Without Inventory: Build Your Dropshipping Empire" serves as your trusted companion on the exciting journey of dropshipping. Packed with practical advice, real-life examples, and valuable insights, this book empowers you to navigate the intricacies of e-commerce with confidence and unlock the true potential of your online business. Get ready to embark on a profitable and fulfilling venture in the world of dropshipping

And as an added bonus, scan the QR code below and get 10% off any t-shirt purchase.

www.ingramcontent.com/pod-product-compliance
Lightning Source LLC
Chambersburg PA
CBHW081157130726
47996CB00009B/3156